first 100 trucks

and things that go

priddy books

airport fire rig

police tow truck

Rescue Vehicles

ladder truck

police boat

rescue rig

fire chief's truck

Coast Guard boat

brush rig

police car

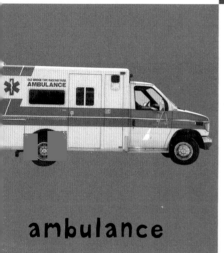

rescue helicopter

ambulance

fire truck

police motorcycle

tractor and baler

tractor and sprayer

tractor and trailer

On the farm

farm pickup

ATV

combine harvester

front loader

tractor

tractor and Seeder

horse truck

tracked tractor

forage harvester

tractor and disc

orklift tractor

backhoe loader

forklift truck

Construction machines

roller

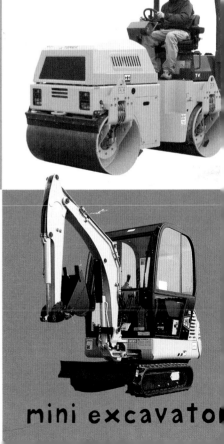

giant excavator

skid steer

crane

mini excavator

excavator

bulldozer

pay loader

dump truck

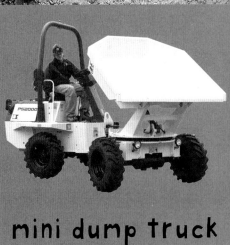

mini dump truck

scraper

cement mixer

motorcycle

container truck

bus

delivery truck

On the road

van

mail truck

car transporter

big rig

scooter

school bus

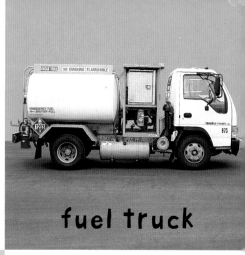

fuel truck

camper van

garbage truck

snowplow

cable repair truck

coupe

taxi

sports car

Cars

race car

vintage car

custom car

Supercar

convertible

4×4

Hummer

pickup

lassic sports car

stretch limousine

family car

hot rod

classic car

tour boat

water taxi

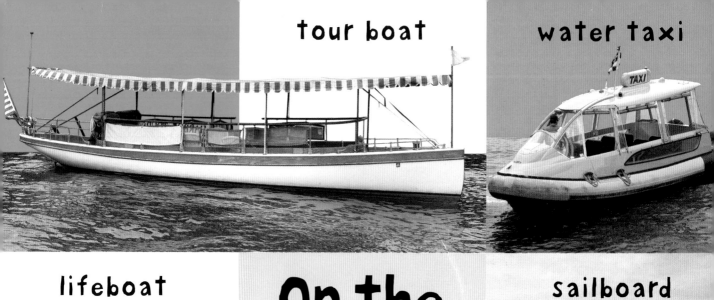

lifeboat

On the water

sailboard

jet ski

speedboat

sailboat

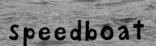

container ship

passenger ferry

fishing boat

motor yacht

canoe

sailing ship

cruise ship

Space Shuttle

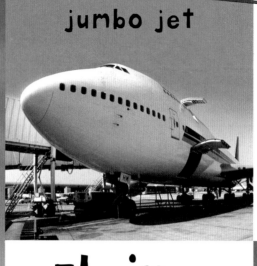

jumbo jet

helicopter

Flying machines

light aircraft

fast jets

passenger jet

hot-air balloon

subway train

passenger train

coal train

on the tracks

commuter train

street tram

monorail

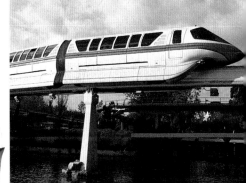

freight train

steam train

What am I?

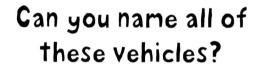

Can you name all of
these vehicles?

Look inside the book
to help!